The Beautiful
—And The—
Broken

by Illiana Cenjur

—*Chapters*—

—Dedication—

*For every weary soul who
has ever felt like life couldn't
possibly get any worse, this
book is for you.*

*It can often seem like there's
no way things will ever get
better. I wrote this book to
remind you that it will, and
to give you some comfort and
hope along the way. May
you find the healing and love
your heart deserves.*

-Illiana Cenjur

—Chapter One—

—Broken Pieces—

i want you to know
that you
with all of your
beautiful
broken pieces

will one day
become
something new
something whole
something new

life will change
the tides will rise and fall
and you
will salvage your hope
piece by piece
from the shipwreck
of past storms

i don't know
if it's as easy
for everyone else
as it looks

but either way
i covet their easy happiness

be with someone
who makes you feel alive
when your spirit is down

he may have broken you
leaving you
without a care

but you
are strong enough
to put yourself
back together

for the soft-hearted lovers
who reach out for love
from those
who would rather
ignore them
to win
some petty game

know that there is someone
out there
who will match your energy
and love you
for who you are
without taking you
for granted

so often in life
we search for love
as something
to be given to us
rather than something
to give
to ourselves

i blame it on the full moon
the way
my love for you
has suddenly
been resurrected

remember this:
the clouds
will always
blow away
with the wind
eventually

don't give up hope

as long as your heart
still beats
you have
a purpose
to fight for

despite my best intentions
i found myself
thinking of you
again

it's not easy
to admit
that you aren't
strong enough
to stop thinking
about
him

do not be afraid
of what others
think of you

be afraid
of being someone
who is so affected
by the opinions of others
that you break yourself down
to fit in their little boxes

sometimes
you have to
let go
in order
to gain

take comfort in the fact
that eventually
your heartache
will fade
and you
will feel whole
again

it's only a matter of time.

first and foremost
you must remember
to be
your own
person

if all you have
is a pretty face
with nothing meaningful
underneath

then you truly
have
n o t h i n g

things might seem
unfair
right now

but don't forget
that karma
always comes around
eventually

brokenness
is not
a curse

it is a blessing,
an opportunity
to put yourself
back together
in a whole new way

do not settle
for anything less
than endless fire
and meadows of butterflies

don't spend one more night
thinking about someone
who is not
thinking
about
you

he may have broken you
but you will rise
beautiful and powerful
from the ashes

most of our relationships
only happen
so we know what
mediocre love
feels like

so that when we taste
the love
of our soul mates
we will know for certain
we have found
the one

you have spent too many
                nights
looking up at the
                stars
hoping for some kind of
                change

when all you had to do
was get up
from your bed
and make it happen
yourself

do not fear
love will always win
in the end

if they don't notice
your absence
they don't deserve
your presence

do not tell
the secrets of your heart
to those
who are careless
with them

be careful
who you vent to

if only it were simple
and i
could easily
stop loving you
even though
you hurt me

sadly
it seems
that the scars
of your love
will never heal

—Chapter Two—

—Love Heals—

there is no salve
so strong
to heal a wounded heart
as love

stay with the one
who looks at you
with awestruck wonder

sadly
some things change
faster than we
are ready
to move on

i miss the way
everything felt
so simple
with you

sometimes
things have to burn
to the ground
before you can build
something new

hope
is not
weakness

hope is the strength
of looking at past
disappointments
and still believing
that life
could get better

there is no greater strength
than to hope

i wish
there was more
i could do
to make you
love me
than just
hope

obsession is unhealthy
but i cannot stop thinking
about you

don't be afraid to fly
everything's scary
the first time

never be afraid
to take time
to take care
of yourself

self love
is a hard fought battle

as long
as you
are determined
to keep going

you have everything
you need

do not give up
just because
you have not yet
found your way
to the other side

you will get there
i promise you.

cherish the people in your life
who are always willing

to give you a shoulder to cry
on

love
is a beautiful salve

romance
stops the pain

but self-love
heals the wounds

things may seem bad
but they won't stay that way

life has its seasons
winter doesn't last forever

as long as you remember that
you will have the strength
to hold on
another day

keep holding on
the darkness will pass
the sun will rise
and everything will be
okay

time will pass
and you will heal

sometimes it feels
like nothing changes

but don't worry
everything does
over time

and that
is a good thing

the darkest times
only make sunny days
look all the brighter

run as fast as you can
into the arms
of love

let it radiate into your heart
and wash away your pain

it's time to let go of the past
it's time to be free

now is your time.

accept yourself
even when you don't see
what there is to love
about yourself

look in the mirror
and know that you
deserve
to be loved

hilliana cenjur

—Chapter Three—

—*Our World*—

do not think yourself
to be any less valuable
compared to others

you are a diamond
among many pearls

though you don't fit in
you are far more valuable
than you could ever imagine

if you find yourself
looking for completion
in someone else

know that if you rely
on others
to feel whole

you will only be
disappointed

our world is painted
in colors of pain

it doesn't have to be this way

reach inwards
for the light
and let it emanate
from within

our society
is more concerned
with the girls
who 'cry wolf'
than the crimes
of the wolves themselves

never settle for a man
who infantilizes you

find someone
who respects you
as your own person

if we allow anyone
to be discriminated against

by what measure
can we defend against such
for ourselves?

you are the light
capable of driving
the darkness
out of our world

nothing can stop you
as long as you
continue to believe
in the power of your soul
to overcome
anything and everything
that befalls you

if you remain silent
and hold back from expressing
what you think is right
then you are a coward

stand for what's right
or don't even bother
        pretending
you're a good person

you do not have to be
defined
by your past mistakes

what a shame it is
that we live in a world
where the right
to not die from sickness
is buried beneath the greed
of billionaires
who want a bigger yacht

hope
never gives up

as long as you
hang on
to hope
and never let go

you will rise
above the stars

know this:

no matter how much hate
there is in the world
the love we share
will always
have
the
last
word

how rare it is
in this world
to have your own opinions

take a stand
for what you believe in

you have nothing to lose
but your comfort

heartbreak
does not teach us
to stop loving

heartbreak
teaches us
that love
is worth
the risk

impossible
is just an excuse
we give ourselves
for not trying
to reach higher
than what's easy

do not tell me
i am hard to love
i wore my scarred heart
on my sleeve
from the very beginning

i have no patience
for people like you
whose only concern
is how they can use me

risk
is what separates
greatness
from mediocrity

do not look
upon the vast cities
full of love stories
and art
and tell me
that humanity
is not something
worth
fighting for

embrace
the things
in life
that make you
feel
outside
your
comfort zone

ultimately we remember our
             lives
in chopped up fragments
in a story
that doesn't quite fit together
so easily and seamlessly
as we expect

nothing can fix our world
except the belief
that things can change
for the better

—Chapter Four—

—Beautiful Scars—

do not dare
look at your scars
and think
that they are ugly

they are beautiful reminders
of battles fought
and the slow progress
you have made
towards healing

why can't you
get
off
my
mind?

it's such a painful irony
that you
brought me
the most happiness
i've ever felt
and also
the most heartbreak

letting go
of you
was the hardest thing
i've ever had
to do

one day
you will find someone
who makes you feel
like life
isn't so bad
after all

our story

i needed it to end

but didn't want it to

i want to give you
e v e r y t h i n g

just because someone
doesn't love you back
doesn't mean
you're not
worth loving

never apologize
for needing
reassurance

how could you expect
someone
to make you happy
in the long run
when they won't even give you
the words you need
right now?

it is all to easy
to need someone to love you
just because they don't

i don't need a view
from a paris rooftop
to fall in love
with you

give me your time
and your words
and gifts of touch

that's all i need

i didn't want to give you
a second chance

but i found myself
giving you
chance after chance
because i wasn't ready
to accept the fact
that we
weren't meant
to be
together

staring at my reflection
in a glass of wine
wondering
what i could have done
to fix us

find someone
who truly understands you
and never let them go

broken souls
create
the most beautiful
love

time
separates us
from the heat of the moment

that can be a good thing
and a bad thing

don't let anyone tell you
you don't deserve
to be
loved

it's impossible
to completely understand
the way
that life
will force you
to change

it is not meant to be
understood
just experienced
and learned from

one day i hope i get to the
point
where i can laugh about you
and about us
instead
of just
crying

you knew my heart was fragile
but you
were willing
to break it
in order to use me
to get what you wanted

i am so ashamed
that i ever let you
near me

love starts
in ways
you never expect it to

and ends
just as unexpectedly

love cannot be predicted

find someone
who is not afraid
to dance
in your fire

i want to be
the book
you read
with the night light on
deep into the night
when you should be sleeping

i hope you never want
to put me down
staying up late
wanting to know more

do not be ashamed
of the mistakes you made
in the past

they were the building blocks
that built you up
into who you are
today

needy and distant
are two words
to describe
two people
out of equilibrium
with each others' needs

find someone
whose arms are wide enough
to hold you
whenever you need it

i want you
even though
you're bad
for me

not every day
can be sunny
or the earth
would be scorched

not every day
in a relationship
can be perfect
or else perfection
would lose its meaning

know that the hard days
can be just as necessary
as the easy days

hope taught me that love is
worth jumping off skyscrapers
for

despair taught me that you
always seem to find the
ground, some skyscrapers are
just higher than others

love taught me that sometimes
jumping off skyscrapers is
worth it for the right person

do not give me a funeral
when i die

turn my body
into ashes
and my ashes
into soil

plant the seeds of roses
and treat them tenderly

turn my end
into new beginnings

i needed it
every time
you told me
you loved me

i'm ashamed of what i did
and what more i would've
done
to make you
keep saying it

there is nothing
quite as bad for you
as going back
to someone
who hurt you

but there's nothing
quite as easy
and comfortable

i guess healing is the art
of being uncomfortable long
enough
to grow past
those
who once held you back

if you want
to look into the heart
of the one you love

look at the way
they treat
perfect strangers

you are not obligated
to become
the person
they say you are

grow beyond their labels
and find
who you truly are

for all the talk
about the stars
controlling our fate

when the time comes
we do not look to them
for guidance

we look
inward
at the cosmos
within us

do not forget
that you
are in control
of your own fate

your love
made me feel
as if i had never
been loved
before

sunshine does not compare
to the light you are
in my life

as long as you remember
to keep your head
above the waves

you will be
alright

when you feel
like you are alone
and no one
understands
what you're going through

know that to struggle
is to be human
and to triumph over struggle
is to grow as a person

they call them 'growing pains'
for a reason

sometimes change hurts
but you have to trust
that it's for the better

we need to focus
on what brings us together
and not
what tears us
apart

don't give anyone the
satisfaction
of getting to define
how you feel about yourself

if you want
to throw everything out
and get
a fresh start

what's holding you back
except fear
that you could be
actually happy?

keep the spotlight
on the positive

never cry
over someone
who would never cry
over you

are are worth far more
than unreciprocated love

life can be more
than half-loves
half-truths
and excuses
not to put it all on the line
in search
of your highest potential

do not surf
on the waves
of trends

find your balance
on the smoothness
of vast waters

do not allow yourself
to be weighed down
by the past

if you allow yourself
to wallow
in past pain

you will not have time
to come up for air

you know you've won
when you begin to realize
that all your pain
has been leading
to something better
than you had before

you deserve someone
who doesn't have to think
about
whether or not
they want to be with you

hold close
and don't let go
to everything
that makes you feel

a l i v e

life is too short
to accept
unfulfilling circumstances
or
unfulfilling relationships

take life in your hands
and shape it
to what you want

—*Thank You*—

Thank you for reading my debut collection of poetry, The Beautiful and The Broken. I hope that it reached you exactly when you needed it most.

Do not forget that you deserve all the happiness you can imagine, and don't settle for anything less.

With all my love ~

-Illiana Cenjur

18887282R00087

Made in the USA
Middletown, DE
02 December 2018